Traumatized

A true story

A family ripped apart by cold-blooded murder

The Lives of Isaiah and Devon Jones

Traumatized

The Lives of Isaiah Jones and Devon Jones

By: Devon Jones

Cover by: Devon Jones

Designed by: Jazzy Kitty Publishing

Logo Designs by: Andre M. Saunders/Leroy Grayson

Editor: Anelda L. Attaway

© 2015 Devon Jones

ISBN 978-0-9970848-0-1

Library of Congress Control Number: 2015959422

All rights reserved. This book is protected under the copyright laws of the United States of America. This book may not be copied or reprinted for commercial gain or profit. The use of short quotations or occasional page copying for personal or group study is permitted and encouraged. Permission will be granted upon request. For Worldwide Distribution. Printed in the United States of America. Published by Jazzy Kitty Publishing utilizing Microsoft Publishing Software. This book is based on a true story "non-fiction" and is public record. At times real names or places have been used. Suggested for mature audience due to graphic details or language. The Holy Scriptures are from the NIV Version of the Holy Bible.

ACKNOWLEDGMENTS

Dear Residents of Wilmington Delaware,

Wilmington Delaware streets have no picks in 2015 and 2016; and it's only going to get worse. Whose family will be next?! It might just be your mom, sister, aunt, dad, uncle, brother, nephew, niece or just your homie. If not, I guarantee before the week is over we're going to hear about one more person getting killed or shot. If you are truly tired of it all, ask yourself…what I can do to make my community a better place?

I'd like to give thanks.

DEDICATIONS

This book is dedicated to Ethelda R. Nuriddin and Benjamin H. Jones.

Also, my family and friends from Raymour and Flanigan.

TABLE OF CONTENTS

INTRODUCTION i

CHAPTER 1 -   The Nightmares 01

CHAPTER 2 -   My Eyes Finally Opened 11

CHAPTER 3 -   The Monsters that Killed My Parents 19

CHAPTER 4 -   Shocked! 25

CHAPTER 5 -   Back to School 30

CHAPTER 6 -   A Family Ripped Apart 40

CHAPTER 7 -   New Evidence 44

CHAPTER 8 -   Suicidal Beginnings 48

CHAPTER 9 -   No Escaping 53

CHAPTER 10 - Mental Slavery 58

CHAPTER 11 - Recognize 66

PHOTOS 76

ADD YOUR OWN SELFIE 77

INTRODUCTION

Have you ever had a nightmare that seemed way too real? A nightmare that feels as if it is happening right then and there?! There are only two explanations for this particular dream. One being that it could just be a figment of your imagination, and the other being that it is absolutely not a dream, but in fact a tragic reality!

Unfortunately, I had to come to the realization that I was not dreaming on one specific night. This one night of all nights was the most horrifying and painful evening that I had ever endured.

On the night of August 31, 2001 at exactly 1:00 am my entire life changed and I didn't blame the Almighty for what had happened. Jesus is my Lord and Savior; He guided me through my valley of the shadows of death. I did fear evil, but I knew He was with me. He comforted me through my pain and He forever will all the days of my life. For without Him I would have shattered into a thousand pieces and melted away in my sorrows. I only had one person to talk to inside my thoughts of the dark void I had because you know that a part of yourself is missing. I only had one person that would understand me because He knew me before I was in my mother's womb. Give all the Glory to God before you enter what it's like to be traumatized. For there is a bigger person to blame in this evil world, which is the Devil. When you work your way up the ranks to who is the one to blame for everything that is happening in our lives, especially for the cries that come out of the Black community it all leads to him. Follow the money trail and it shows you all the key players that led up to August 31, 2001. The drug money that caused this nightmare is pumped into the Black community from our very own government to support everything that you love about the greatest country in the world. It's all corrupt because they made billions and billions of dollars off Black lives. First, being the bloodshed and broke tree branches of slavery. Second, the war on drugs that still feeds on our communities like leaches to fragile skin. The fact of the matter is I thought I was traumatized by what I witnessed. But the truth is I was traumatized by just being born into this world. We are all traumatized, but the sad thing is you don't know it yet and this is why.

Traumatized

CHAPTER 1

The Nightmares

Trapped inside the inner 4 walls of my mind is a 14-year-old boy. The boy is me and no matter what, I can't escape this room I built. Similar to the forts children build to keep out the monsters that lurk deep in the thick darkness of crying souls. This fort has no doors, no windows, and without air I'm drowning in tears. If you asked how I get locked in here. And if you only knew, then you would be locked in here with me.

The world is full of evil and everybody in it is only out to take what you have. Regardless of where I live, the world is outside these walls. These walls have a name and "Wilmington Delaware" is embedded in its insulation. The fibers are the city that is so corrupt that it doesn't even understand why its' fabricated with no respect for a human life. Google my name, but you won't find me, I'm invisible like oxygen. I'm an important element as I bring life, joy, laughter, and happiness to the people who know me. Too bad it's just a pretty wrapping paper I placed on my mind captivating structure.

The moment of walking out of my tiny bedroom to get a bite to eat haunts my dreams every night. Hearing slow steps as the old wood cracks beneath their feet, coming closer towards me whispers through the air. My voice calls out to loved ones as I assume it's them. But, why would they be moving with no sense of urgency to get to their destination? My words get no reply as they echo off the hallway into the open bathroom door facing adjacent the stairs. Inching out towards the unfamiliar noises a hand appears. This is the moment that your mind begins to place you in your own spiritual fortress. The movement that is so real that you can't believe this is about to happen to you, out of all people. You do this to protect yourself mentally and emotionally. Now, my heart begins to fill with fear to only beat rapidly out of my chest. The hand goes out of sight, and then the stocking cap covered nightmare appears. Why couldn't it have been the boogie man or Jason Voorhees? I would have had a better time seeing them because I know they are not as real as the moment here.

"9-1-1, what is your emergency?" was the only voice I want to come into my small ear from the sound of the dispatcher on the other side of the telephone? She patiently listens as she hears deep breathing and the sound of the gunfire roar through the telephone. I was lucky enough to manage to quickly swing the door shut as this monster tried to kick my door down as I braced myself between the door and the bunk bed behind me. *"Please come quickly,"* replayed outside and in my thoughts. I'm now putting myself in my four cornered trauma shield and as I yell, screams are unheard.

While this young boy with my name is still trapped and torn. So he can tell his story to show how crime in Wilmington needs to end now. We don't need any more little Devon Jones's being traumatized by the horrific tragedies of inner city life. There is so much sorrow to go around in the Black community. You can easily evolve into a bitter person with no emotion by surrounding yourself with like-minded individuals who are called sperm donors because "father" would be too great of a name. So why should they care? Wilmington is their caged environment and in the jungle it gets tough when you have to rob another man because your children's puppy dog eyes look at you because they haven't eaten all day. And you can't find an employer based on the ridiculous choices you made as a young adolescent. Yeah, I understand, but why are you on East 23rd in a place I thought was my safe haven. Until you forced me a reason to believe otherwise.

All this is floating through my thoughts as they're right on the other side of the door. The words fell off my tongue while I'm bathing in distressed fear. The dispatcher tried to calm me down so that she could ask me my address. 1-0-5 flashes in my mind pulsating like hazard lights as the numbers came out in a quick stutter.

My 10-year-old brother is sitting on the bottom bunk bed glaring at me. Isaiah watches me slip in and out of mental consciousness, as my eyes shift from left to right. He cries because he hears nothing, but loud thumping and scuffling noises in the hallway. I'm so nervous and a warm stream of urine trickles down my legs. Our adolescent minds try to interpret all the noise that is vibrating through the walls. The sounds of moaning are coming from the other side of the door. Holding this white wooded barrier closed so that the nightmares don't seep in and kill me and Isaiah. A look of confusion on his face as his light complexion fades. I start to scream so loud that my ears begin to ring. I didn't know what was going to happen to us. We will never see tomorrow, let alone the next 10 minutes? If this masked monster fires his 9mm handgun through this door, my life force will escape my body. Then they will most likely pump one into my little brother's head. Who will even know we are gone from this world if we would have been killed? They wouldn't have found us all until one of my older brothers or sisters came by the house to check up on us. I guess it's possible to die even though you are alive. Your mind just faces the fact that you are going to die, so it prepares your body for it. For me, I died this rainy August night and when it was over I never woke up.

Still stuck in time at the age of fourteen and the world around me is my Neverland while Captain Hook and his group of gold robbing bandits are invading my home. There is the smell of hot metal, gun smoke that escapes from the hallway into my nostrils. And my mother and fathers' room was not even two inches from ours.

While I'm holding the door with my back on the door, my size seven feet pushed off the second step of the ladder of our bulk bed. I can't completely close the door because of the City Blue sneaker bag that we were using to put trash in, prevented that from happening.

Glancing over the top of our dark mahogany bulk bed with Ninja Turtle covered mattresses I can see the second entrance that connected their room and ours. It was blocked by a stack of clothes that filled moving boxes. We had just moved into the house not even a month ago. We all were fixing the house by putting up new dry wall and electrical outlets. There was still so much work to be done because the house had not been updated since my grandfather brought the house in the 1940's.

I remember stories of my mother telling me that they were the only Black family that lived on this street until our opposite colored counterparts slowly started to move out of Wilmington. Because having Black people in your neighborhood lowers the property value of your home. They moved out of the city into their brand new suburban homes that were being built in Hockessin, Newark and Middletown. Giving out their homes to the Section 8 of the Housing Act of 1937 that authorizes the payment of rental HOUSING ASSISTANCE to private landlords on behalf of approximately 4.8 million low-income households as of 2008.

That way they could make money off of the new Black community that was forming in inner city Wilmington. They would make the rent twice as high because they knew that the government would pay for most of it. Till this day, our family home on East 23rd Street is the only house not owned by Section 8. White families get to make money hand over fist as they can bank their money that they're making off their DuPont jobs. While this community turns into the scum of the bottom of the barrel.

And the fact is that while you're on Section 8 you have to stay at certain annual income and no father figure can be listed living in the household. Leading to a downward spiral of children born without loving fathers or leadership. And without leadership in the home, a child has a high probability of becoming the very people that are in my home at this second.

I have tunnel vision in those boxes on the opposite side of our blue printed colored room. My parents' television flashes through the cracks. Night dreaming that the nightmare out there could plow its way into my parents' bedroom and knock that stack down like some sort of Godzilla movie. Only to have bullets whistle in the air into my little brother's temporal lobe. Brain filled blood splatter oozes out of his lifeless body as he slides half from on the bed onto the floor. Then the second shot hits my chest, burning through me, feeling my heart beat stop and I gasp from the blood that fills my lungs. Falling down onto the floor, only to let the nightmare in to put two more shots into our skulls to make sure we were really dead.

Visualizing your own death is even scarier than facing the reality that is really happening in front of you. What people fail to realize is that if you go through a traumatizing experience like molestation, rape or a train derailment on an Amtrak track. It's not what is happening to you in real time that is putting you in a state of complete shock. The shock is what you are imagining is going to happen to you as you're experiencing something tragic. You are living your future in your mind and you haven't even done it yet and when it doesn't happen the way you thought it would happen you become stuck between your imagination and reality. I'm stuck in between imagination and reality and the Lord is my straw allowing me to have air as I'm in this dark hole filled with creatures that lurk in the darkness. If you ever tried to breathe through a straw? I dare you to try it. You will have enough air to live, but not enough to function for a long period of time. I'm suffocating in fear as I try to escape my thoughts, but this is the start of my depression. Forever trying to gasp for air, but finding it will never come and you wish you would die because you think that will help you escape this living nightmare.

Where is the police? They are taking way too long. The sweat that is rolling off my forehead into my eyes is drying up faster than they can show up. The police don't come quickly in Wilmington. Don't forget that the money hungry politicians don't want to spend more money to help keep the city of Wilmington safe. It's a lot cheaper just to let the Black monkeys that they call us to kill ourselves. If I was in those nicer neighborhoods like I seen on the old black and white Andy Griffin shows that you see on Nick at Night, and then maybe we have a chance to live to see the sun rise in the morning.

"Can you see what's going on?" the dispatcher said. *This bitch on the phone doesn't care about us. Why would she want me to look into the darkness that haunts my dreams at night? Why is she asking me this ridiculous question? Why does this even matter at this time of distress? The only thing that matters is my address that these police officers are taking way too long to get to.* That thought never leaked out of my mouth and instead I told her, "All I can see is my father's hairy toe."

Pain aching cries echo off the floral covered wall papered walls in the hallway. I can't figure out if it was my father cries that was from my mother's bloody corpse that lies on his chest with her head over his shoulder. Her hair was thick and matted from the blood that seeped deep into her dark brown curls like it was conditioner. Can you imagine knowing that you just lost the love of your life after fourteen years and three kids later? Feeling that pain is even worse than the burning bullet wounds that he was feeling coming from of his own body. "Please come quick," is what I kept telling her. Hoping the more I say it, the faster the police would show up.

I tried to stay as calm as possible and to be strong for my little brother Isaiah. But, that didn't work; I couldn't stop the tears from tickling the tiny hairs running down my face as adrenaline rushes through my body. Everything is going in slow motion, every second feels like a full minute. Your 5 senses increase in sensitivity. I could hear the heavy raindrops outside my window when rushing down our gutters into a slow leak that drizzle down our window pane. I watched the window fog up from the screams of terror. Through the horrific insanity that is going on at the moment.

I just began to thank God for allowing my mother to put a telephone in my room. Always watching shows like Full House and Rebecca would ask her father for a phone in the room so that she could talk to her friends or future boyfriend. I had no friends to talk to in school; I just thought it would be a good thing to have in my room. Unfortunately, I never got to use the white wired phone with the glow in the dark buttons for the purpose a pit was intended. Instead, I'm using it because my nightmare is trying to take us out this world. A week ago I asked my mother and she almost said no and if that telephone had not been in the room, this 911 call would not even be going on. Remember, everything happens for a reason and we were not meant to die that day on August 31, 2001. It wasn't meant for 4 bodies to be buried in Grace Lawn Cemetery in New Castle, Delaware.

The dispatcher told me the police are downstairs and to go down and open the door for them. When I use to tell people what this lady told me to do, they would look at me in disbelief. Do you see where our hard working tax money goes into training people that make suggestions like this? Maybe she wanted me to blindly walk out and get shot. Till this day it is still the dumbest request I ever had person tell me. If I could only jump into the sound waves of the telephone and through the phone lines like Freddie Kruger did on Nightmare on Elm Street. My fist would collide with her mandibular joint and cause it to shatter. So that she would have some common sense to never tell a fourteen old boy this again. I told her to just have the police kick the front door down and get us out of here. I mean, what were they doing down there knocking the whole time like solicitors. Who trained these people? Oh yeah, I forgot this is Wilmington's finest police officers who swore to protect and serve. Maybe they hoped ever one was dead inside so they wouldn't have to do their jobs.

"*This nightmare is almost over maybe they will catch them in the act,*" *I thought.* "They will be right up to get you out of there," she said on the phone. This quick couple of minutes seemed like an hour. "Ok their downstairs!" I answered loudly to be sure who everyone was on the other side of the door could hear me holler.

By the time the police got there the criminals had already left. They left and bloody white tee shirt behind that was hanging out the back bedroom open window. And the fresh drywall that we just put in that back room was now soaked with cold rain coming from the window being open. The light from the police flashlights shined through the crack of our door onto the nearby wall where our television was located. I heard the police say. "Who's in there? Come out now!" *I'm thinking, "Are you serious right now? Who do you think is in here?"* So I get down from the position that I was in to slowly open the door. The door creaks open and my little brother five feet and two-inch structure is standing right beside me at this point. Slowly, I watched the police officer service weapon appear through the threshold. His weapon was pointed right in Isaiah's face as if he was going to give him a point blank kill shot in his forehead. My arm quickly swats the officer's gun down from my brother's face as we come out the room with our hands up. The police dragged Isaiah and me out the blue fortress that we mentally built for ourselves to keep the nightmares out. Sure enough, the nightmare was out here because it left its bread crumb evidence of its existence.

If you were our age at the time and you saw what we had seen at this eye opening moment, what would you do? Would you break down and cry only to kneel down over top of the two strongest support systems you ever knew? Saturating their skin with your sorrow as you wished they would just wake up embracing you with a loving hug. Telling you that everything is fine and we will be okay. Only in movies do silly endings happen, so that the audience has a chance of relief. There are no happy endings in the real world. Very few people die in their sleep in peace as the Lord takes them to their heavenly place. Most will die in some type of pain, whether it be cancer, aids, heart attack or whatever. All you can do is pray that the pain isn't the pain my parents felt while being gunned down by the nightmare.

We stepped over our parent's bloody vessels. The Wilmington Police had already lifted my mother's body off my father. They placed their lifeless corpse's shoulder to shoulder. The police checked their risk for vital signs with their two fingers. At the time, I didn't believe that they were even dead. I looked at their faces trying to read any sign of any emotion deep down passed their cold skin into their soul. Staring at my mother's face and all she had on was her big long white shirt with a gray dog on it and nothing down, but her panties she was wearing. Her light skinned complexion started to turn to a pale white as the blood was leaking out of her into the nooks and crannies of the wood floor. The pool of blood that was pouring out of our father's body was so thick as if it was dark red cherry yogurt. The only thing that was warm in this dark hallway was the hot air that was coming out of my parents' room from the fan they had in the window. This night will forever be in our minds until the day we leave this earth. Physically, but mentally we had already left and will be forever scarred.

CHAPTER 2
My Eyes Finally Opened

Now at the age of 28-years-old my eyes are finally open to see the world for what it really is. Nothing but violence, hate and people trying to do whatever it takes to survive. Whether we decide to find a way to survive in violence or no violence. We have to make sure we make the right choices because a life can depend on it or in my case. The life of two people that meant a lot to the people around them. There's no more late night phone calls checking up on mom to see what she doing. Instead, it's substituted by a Dial tone after the beat. Constantly, listening to the voicemail message over and over just to hear the sound of her voice. Bringing back memories that make you smile as salty tear drops run down your cheeks ending at your chocolate lip. There is no more playing basketball with your dad at the Kingswood Park over Riverside. Watching him bounce the ball as you see the joy in his face as he plays the game he loved the most. Only to be replaced by empty courts and homeless men sitting on urinated park benches as I ride by in my Honda Civic. Old smiles turn to new tears as the memories become my DeLorean time machine. There's no Doc Brown to take me back to the past as his Marty Mcfly. I blame Black pride and ignorance to not excel past their ratchetness. Thinking the world, they live in is all about the next Jordan's that is coming out or what Meek Mills will say next in his beef battle against Drake. Too lazy to rise above it all not knowing that there is more to life than just finding the next Dutch Master, and finding someone to match the amount of weed they have with them. It makes them feel good to gossip and pick fights just to post to Worldstar Hip Hop or Facebook for likes and comments from their mutual friends.

Black communities raise more demons in angel clothing than any other community and the worst part is that you accept it. You hear about murders just about every day from Delaware online and it becomes numb. For example, on July 24, 2015 a woman's body was found on a sliding board in Wilmington's Canby Park. The body could be seen at the top of the red plastic slide in a playground area that sits within view from Union Street and Prospect Road, close to where the park stretches out into New Castle County. The body was that of a heavyset woman with what appeared to be blood on her upper body and clothing at her ankles. Police officers draped a yellow tarp over the slide's top platform to shield the body from view and cordoned off the park and adjoining parking lot with yellow plastic tape. A 911 call at 10:30 a.m. reported a suspicious man in the park, between the 600 block of S. Union St. and 700 block of S. Lincoln St. Responding officers discovered the woman's body, she said. Imagine if you sent your child outside to play at the park and going up the slide they found a murder victim. Poor babies would be traumatized for the rest of their lives and as a parent, there's nothing you can do to make that image in their mind go away.

Wilmington, Delaware used to be a place where you could be somebody. At least that's what the old wooded sign on Concord Pike use to say. So when did it change to the place where you can get shot by pill popping gangsters that will take pictures of your brain matter coming out of your skull as your body turns cold form the winter snow? Then post it on Instagram for all of social media to see; to think that your last picture couldn't even have been you dressed up in your Sunday's best with a nice smile on your face enjoying life with your loved one. Instead, your last picture is for someone else's twisted amusement. No, not everybody is a monster in Wilmington, but how do you know? Nobody ever thinks that their child is capable of doing such a thing. So it makes it so much harder to believe. How could my honor student be a ruthless murder capable of killing a whole family? This makes you think long and hard of the why and how. It's simple everybody has a shell that they reveal to the world. But, instead, you tend to be a totally different person on the inside. Somebody that only you know and you fight with that man or woman every day. People influence the inner person inside of you because you feed off their energy. It's a rush to do something you know you're not supposed to be doing. These young boys out here feeling like you in some kind of gangster movie like Shottas' or Belly. But, when you do the impossible you may not even know what you have done because in your mind you're still living the movie. Telling the world fuck that I ain't do it and nobody better not snitch. I look at you on First 48 and call you a fool. Sitting down in on that hard chair in a cold closet size room. You're trapped in the illustrative images in your flap book movie that you have made up in your mind. So why live in a movie? Why pretend to live a lifestyle that you take a life of another person. Forcing children that live in your own neighborhood to live with no parents or guidance because you took it away. When your parents are gone you are forced to live with other people who barely know you and if you messed up one time you get tossed aside. They are the first ones to say maybe you should go live with your sister or your brother. Like you're some kind of pet and because you have been so disobedient they figure they take you to the dog pound.

Lying on a cold cemented floor with the smell of old urine left from the other dogs. That was locked up in this wire fence dog cage like you are mental. Feeling like an animal for so many years, but it wasn't my fault at all. A common mind would say fuck the world and everything in it. I don't care if your mom is a junky living in the clouds as the prick of the needle head punctures her skin. Injecting the sweet poison into her veins. She can give ten-dollar blow jobs to the truckers that come though on New Castle Avenue. It's a bigger problem here in this city has to be fixed. Love is the only emotion that matters in this reality. Show love for everyone regardless if they talk about us in front of our face or behind our back. Show love to ourselves so you can love others. Show love so that jealousy, hate, and pride don't cloud our mind. Shower in love so that our body, mind and soul can become hydrated by it. We cannot let our love tank run dry by Wilmington. Wilmington depends on it. I'm going to hurt you because I feel hurt inside; which most of the time this is the case. Wilmington took them away from me, but I can't show hate towards my city. It's just infected with a disease called hate and its venom flows in the veins of the youth of this city. They don't want the love anti-venom because they are afraid that it will make them weak and vulnerable. This problem in Wilmington is so big. According to the Mayor or the City Council in Wilmington. Nobody knows how to fix the issue. Might as well call this our geological algebraic equation. Because we all know that for some people math is a difficult subject to master. But, I don't care how long it takes to get fixed, as long as something is done. Otherwise, I'll still be trapped in the thoughts of my deep depression. Constantly going back and forth between nightmares and the world. Sitting here in a daze as everything goes through my mind like the flow of water to the time of when the police escorted us out of our house of horror on East 23rd Street. There were at least ten police cars and one ambulance outside that stretched out about a block long. The red and blue lights lit up the whole block like Christmas decorations.

The EMT's (Emergency Medical Team) rushed past us as the Wilmington Police Officers turned every single light on in the house. One hundred eyes focusing on us outside to witness nothing, but trying to understand what had gone on in our home. I felt their thoughts reaching into the deep corners of my mind. We have just turned into the conversation of the night into the next morning. As if we were part of some type of creep show putting on a show for their entertainment. Hearing the whispers float off their lips through the air under the sound of police sirens. If Facebook were around in 2001 this would have been posted on your mutual friends' walls. Constantly commenting and putting in their two cents as if it's worth anything. Quickly followed by an urgent post from Delaware Crime Stoppers. Asking for any information for leads on some possible suspects. Too bad it wouldn't have been any comments on that post because Black people are too afraid to speak up, but claim they want the violence to stop in the inner city.

The sole of my bare feet pressing downward on loose pebbles and old cracked sides walks. Feeling sharp pains from its tiny ridges moving up my spine. Sadly, Isaiah and I were not the type children that went to bed with pajama and slippers on. We like to go to bed with nothing, but our cartoon character underwear on. We waited inside the police car half naked wondering why these seats are so uncomfortable. The cars had these rock hard plastic seats and no seat belts, similar to the seats they have in bumper cars. The car reeked of burnt crack rocks and sweaty ass crack as if they just got done dropping off some junky in Gander Hill. Why would they put two young children in this type of police vehicle? At the moment, I didn't care I just wanted to get out from around my house. I just kept staring into the open doorway from the inside of this vehicle as if my house was haunted.

 Fourteen-year-old Devon was held captive by the diabolical demons that left their essence drifting deep down under the bloody floor boards. Seeing my ghostly body standing in the entry way. His bloodshot eyes were staring into my beating heart. Fear caused me to leave a part of myself behind. Forever running because you're too afraid to go back and collect what you lost yourself. I no longer want to live in that moment in time. So I tried to erase it and lock it away in my subconscious. Being out in the open, I knew the killer was standing around looking at us in the crowd. The nightmares are pretending to be a normal onlooker just waiting for its' chance to finish the job. The police officer that put us in the car waited to leave us and you screamed to the top of lungs for him to stay by the car with us because our minds were deeply soaked in fear by what we just witnessed.

 I was so happy when the officer finally started his engine and started to move after ten minutes of waiting. We never been around the city before because we never been anywhere without our father. I had no idea where we were going or where I was at. All I know is that we ended up at this building with a huge gate and we got out the smelly car and walked in the building. Instant goose bumps came all over our unclothed bodies. Our bodies tense up to conserve heat and while our bottom lip began a fast shiver.

We could have got sick just being in the police station. It the middle of summer, but Jack Frost lived in here as he played with the fine hairs on my back. I asked the officer. Why it is so cold in here?" He replied, "Because we are required to have at least three layers of clothing. A white under shirt, bullet proof vest, and then our uniform. It can be really hot in all this, so we need it cool in here so we have to relax in summer months." I said to the police officer, "Is there any way that we can get some clothes to put on because it's really chilly in here." If I didn't ask we all can assume that the police officer would let us be as we were, which was half naked in Ninja Turtle underwear. "Sure," the officer said. So he contacted somebody from the Emergency Department at the hospital down the street and they brought us some medical scrubs and booties for our feet.

It's 3:00 in the morning and this officer is writing his report and he can't even get the ages right. But, I was sitting right next to him. Police in Wilmington couldn't care less. Murders happen all day long. So in his mind this is a typical, normal day like waking up in the morning to put on your shoes. I just remember trying to stay up until the sun came up and being jacked up on caffeine from the ultimate of soda that they allowed us to have.

We ended up in this big conference room watching the Cartoon Network, waiting patiently until the police got in touch with my older sister to pick us up. A thought comes across my head and I don't think I could process it all and I still don't think I have until this very day. I really didn't know what to think. If it wasn't for my dad taking us to church and knowing about prayer, I don't think I would have had such a sound mind. I was praying for that they would make it out okay and that we will go home.

At this point, it is 6:00 in the morning and the birds were beginning to chirp outside. We were so tired that we felt like zombies. Like we were awake, but asleep. So I turned to my right and looked over my shoulder as the chair I was sitting in squeaked while in mid swivel. A chrome door knob turned slowly while the creaky door opens. It was my Sister Diwanya and her husband, Donald Deputy. My older sister was just about the only phone number I knew. It's wasn't like it is today with iPhones 6s that can store thousands of numbers. We had to remember a phone number by heart. When she sat down, she was crying so much and I knew it wasn't good news that we were going to hear. They were accompanied by a woman. She informed my little brother and me that my mother had been shot in the back of her head and she died instantly. At the moment, my heart stopped and I looked down and my legs began to shake. She also told us that my father was shot in the neck and in the shoulder and he is currently in the ICU. "What's ICU?" I asked. "Intensive Care Unit," she replied. So many thoughts ran through my mind, but I didn't know how to think. All I knew is that my legs wouldn't stop shaking. I didn't know if I was doing it out of shock or shaking because I wanted to put on a show like I did feel something. Trying to hold the tears back I looked over at Isaiah and his head was on his resting on the table as tears soaked into the veneers. The pain was so deep for him and his journey at his age of twenty-four ended up being a lot worse than mines.

CHAPTER 3

The Monsters that Killed My Parents

I can label the men that killed my parents as monsters. The nightmare that you dream at night can't even compare to what we've seen!

The hardwood floors in the upstairs hallways had to be replaced because the blood soaked into the wood and caused it trickle down into the kitchen below. Yes, only a monster can do such a thing, but can we label them as monsters? Maybe these men are just lost and this is the only way they know. Maybe there was no father figure to show them a different way. Sometimes its mothers out here in Wilmington that ain't worth two shits anyway.

I remember when I was 21-years-old; I had a friend and we use to sell a little of drugs back then. I was just playing out in the streets just to see what the lifestyle was like. I didn't really think about if I got caught or at the worst died in the act of me doing so. On the other hand, for my friend it was a lifestyle that he was forced to live. One day we were riding around doing deliveries for Gino's Pizza on Market Street. In between the stops we had to stop by his house because he forgot his jacket. He invited me into his house as he ran upstairs to get his jacket. As soon as we walked in the door his mom was coming out of the kitchen with her pink curlers in her nappy head. The smell of weed smoke deodorized the dirty blue robe and it got stronger the closer she came to the front door. The first thing that comes out of her mouth was, "How much you make out there?" At this moment my mind was blown away. She was forcing her child to go out and hustle because she was too lazy to work and she wanted to live off Section 8 and Government Assistance. He loved his mother so much that he would risk his life to make sure she was taken care of, to the point that he might just kill a man to do so. At the same time, the number one woman in his life he hardly had any respect for. So how could he ever have respect for another person or better yet another female? In his mind woman ain't shit and I might as well pay my little five dollars for a four-dollar nick bag and ninety-nine cent Dutchy. Ask her to come chill and smoke with me so I can get her relaxed and fuck her. Who cares if she turns out pregnant, I ain't taking care of no baby cause ain't nobody take care of me. Ask yourself this, if you were forced to grow up like my friend was would you even know you was a monster or would you think it's normal? You don't know what it's like to live on the other side of the fence. I didn't understand why somebody would kill my parents. Until this day, when I realized that the things you go through in this world can make you do the unthinkable.

I stopped selling drugs after that; it just wasn't in me. I guess I was doing it just to fit in and it felt good to be able to relate to someone beyond my family problems. This roller coaster of a life of mines forces me to live in my past memories, but never in the present. I'm forever that little 14-year-old boy trapped in my bedroom. Dealing with the world as if I have Alzheimer's and if my fiancée talks to me she has to say it twice for me to hear her. That makes her angry, but I just wish she'd understand what being a victim feels like.

Lying down on my King size bed and as my head hit the pillows and my eyes become heavy I jump back in time to after we left the police station and headed down Governor Printz back to my sister's house. At this time, she lived in Edgemoore Gardens, Apt 3C. The whole ride I tried to rest my eyes, but I couldn't. Too afraid that when I went to sleep, I would never wake up. The morning made my eyes hurt feeling like a vampire. Getting out her 2003 Honda Accord my legs felt like I had cement shoes on. The three flights of stairs took us forever to get up. Listening to the sound of washing machines run on the bottom floor as Tide Laundry Detergent freshened my nose from the gun smoke that tingled my hairs. Walking through her front door of her apartment was the beginning of a new life for me. I locked the door behind me and I found myself starring at the locks on the door. Trying to make sure that I'm visually sure the door is locked. I even tried to push it to make sure I heard the door click. Throughout the day, I did this because I guess deep down I felt like it was my fault our attackers got into our home. Maybe I left the door unlocked and that is how they got in just kept playing over and over in my mind. My mind was playing tricks on me making me feel like it was my fault, even though I knew that it wasn't. I guess me checking the door like that made me feel safe.

We walked down the hall into the bedroom where my nephews and niece were and they were up watching cartoons. And they looked at us as we walked in and they asked us what we were doing here. We rarely came over our sister Diwanya's house. The only time we came over was if my mom and dad wanted time by themselves. So we being there was a total surprise because normally they would come over our house. Mostly because we always had the best toys and games. It was cool because we were all around the same age. That's what happens when your mother has nine children and then those children have children. My sister told my two nephews and my little niece what happened. They were in shock because they said that they were planning to come over. If they had, who knows how that would have played out? Protecting myself and Isaiah was more than enough for me. My niece was 4-years-old back at that time and she was up against the wall sitting down with her head on her knees crying. She had just lost the only grandmother, she ever known. They not only took my mother and father from me, but took their grandmother. No more Sunday dinners filled with fried chicken, macaroni and cheese, and greens with corn bread on the side. Everybody knows a grandmother always makes the best meals and give you all the best love. I knew how she felt because I only had one living grandmother, which was my father's mother Gloria. I always was envious of my friends in school because they always had all four of their grandparents and I only had one. Now my niece has none, so she is even worse off than I was. As she cried, I looked at her with confusion because she was crying. I didn't understand how she even knew what she was crying for, but she did. Amazing even at 4-years-old she understood what happened, but I didn't. Till this day I still haven't really cried over my parents' murder. Somehow I have numbed myself not feel any emotion. I put a wall up so that nothing can hurt me. Fear of heart hurting pain holds all of your tears back. So you try not to think about it at all. People may think that not feeling anything is a bad thing. For some that might be, but for me it helped me get through things. I can now look into peoples' eyes and understand how they feel. Sometimes I can almost feel what they are thinking about. This why I help people the way I do. I am such a humble person that I can clearly think about peoples' feelings and make a judgement. I believe the numbness is a gift God has given me to cope. Without the numbness I could have been a completely different

Traumatized

Devon.

By this point, so far I have been up for a total of 48hrs. I was praying for protection and that this will never happen again in my life. I don't know if I can handle two dramatic events in my lifetime. As I laid there a thought came in my mind. Something was telling me that my parents were going to visit me tonight. I was so scared of the thought of that. More afraid than I was at the scene of the crime. I told the Lord, I don't think I can handle seeing them as a free spirit in front of me. If they had to come say something to please let them come in my dreams. So after that I instantly fell asleep. In the dream I was back in the house on 23rd Street and I was sitting on the floor in front of my mother. She had on a blue shirt and white Capris with flower on them and her brown sandals that she got from Strawbridge's before they turn into Macys. While she had her blue travel bag with the wheels on it. She would use this bag if she was going on vacation. Normally go to my brother older brother Tony's house in Virginia. He used to take her ever mother for a week and pamper her. She loved it when Mother's Day came around because that was her oasis. In this dream I couldn't speak, but she was talking to me. *"Everything will be just fine,"* she said to me as she was sitting on the bottom bunk bed in *my room with tears was coming down her face. I got up from the floor and looked out the window. I see my father putting bags in a U-Haul truck. Then he stopped what he was doing and looked at me and waved.* What I could take from this dream that they were telling me that they were moving on to a better place.

The next few weeks were kind of one big blur? All until the funeral day and going out with my cousins to go out and pick out clothes for the funeral. That next day we woke up and there were two Limos outside. I remember being so excited just riding in a Limo. As a child growing up in the ghetto you don't experience certain things that other people more fortunate would have. It's a shame my first time riding in a Limo couldn't have been going to prom or taking a beautiful woman on an unforgettable date. That she will never forget for the rest of her life. My first time was going to my parents' funeral; calling shotgun before Isaiah so that I can get the front seat. When I got in the Limo. I remember at awe about of nice and clean this stretch Lincoln Town Car was. When we showed up to the viewing, all my family was there. It was like a family reunion to me that everyone showed up dressed up for. Remember, the numbness is still running through me. I don't feel anything emotional in any type of way. I'm just being a kid having fun and experiencing something new in my life with no sense of reality of what is really going on. Watching my mother and father lying in their caskets was so surreal. It didn't seem like they were dead. It seemed as if they were sleeping and that they would just wake up. Just to tell us we can go home and go on with the rest of our day. I couldn't even cry because I didn't know what was going on. It was a regular day to me, but the one thing I did promise myself is that I don't want to go to anymore funerals. I would rather remember a person for who they were. I don't want my last memory of a person not alive. The funeral was September 7, 2001.

CHAPTER 4

Shocked!

When your family is shocked by an earthquake of information. Peaceful sleeping at night with your hair wrapped tight; dreaming about the next day and hoping it was better than yesterday. Only to be woken up by a phone call at 3:00 am that your brother, your mom, and your father have been shot dead and they are currently at the Christiana Hospital. That is the moment a piece of yourself crumbles and turns to dust as your stomach turns from the void that been placed on your heart. The world is not the same as it was yesterday. The bullshit that went on at your job or school you would rather relive that day than your current moment. The moment is so horrific that you have family from both sides standing in a room of silence and tears. Nobody is talking, but everybody is thinking the same thing, *"This is not real I know my God will make a way."* While hoping the impossible becomes possible, but if it doesn't you lose faith in the Almighty as if it's His fault. He didn't make the weed smoke passing through their lung passages manipulating their mind as the E&J relaxes their body to fade away the pain that they feel in everyday Wilmington. Influenced by their lifestyle to kill other people to only make them feel the pain that they feel inside.

We all have a choice and that is not God fault. Blaming the Almighty for a devilish act is foolish. But, we do it because we think about ourselves and our hurts and our pains and nobody else matters at this moment of time. *My beloved is laying on this hospital bed fighting for their life as they walk freely in the streets.* Those thoughts pass in your mind over and over, while mixed emotions don't blend well. Deep sorrow turns to hate towards who ever feels differently than you. Believe me, is all a trick that you think they are running free. If they were free, do you think they would feel the need to live in a lifestyle that only they know? They feel trapped in a world of hate as they go to sleep at night putting cotton balls in their ears so the roaches can't lay eggs inside them as they sleep. If you call that free, but to me it sounds like hell. Too bad the family does think like me because remember they're only thinking about themselves and sitting in silence as the room is filled with tears. Moments like these tears families apart. Reason being, is because everybody is thinking, but nobody is talking. The glue that brings the family together is now dead and gone from this earth, but you can't find new glue? Family's should separate they should be closer, but they are not. My Uncle Glenn always felt pain throughout his whole life, but he didn't place harm to anybody else just his self. Back and forth to rehab, but never being fully rehabilitated. One day his emotions finally came out and he talked about how he felt inside. On our way to Philadelphia my Cousin Rubal and I picked him up cause we seen him walking the hard streets on Philly as he babysitted his dollar keystone that helped him coupe from his current situation. We head to my Cousin Net's home on the outside of town finding ourselves on her sheet cover couch. He talked about home a lot and how he missed my father as warm tears run down his cheeks. Voice in slow cracked tone as his sickness he was suffering from felt heavier from pain he was feeling. He said to me Devon I have nothing and if you live with me I promise I stop what I'm doing to myself. Knowing that you would be a reminder of him would give me life. Looking into his light brown dilated pupils I could see his pain on truth that was pouring out of his soul. Wanting to say yes to his request, but looking away to my cousin Net's reaction on her face as her head shook with a no. Forced me to say no in a nice way to not make him feel even worse about himself. Only to find that months later he finally died from the hurt and pain that he felt all his life from living with my grandmother Gloria and my father's death. When death happens in the family nobody wants to talk about it because the hurt is so deep that nobody wants to bring up repressed emotions. Imagine the wave of emotions my Uncle Mike had to feel watching his older brother lay there as IVs attached with medical tape clinging to his bruised arms. Listening to the sound of heart monitors beep in a constant rhythm. His indescribable face swollen from bullet wounds left in his body. How could he look at him with love knowing that this image will forever be engraved in his mind? The doctor is coming in giving the news the he would be brain dead for the rest of his life. All the family had to agree to take him off life support and you feel guilty killing the person you love the most. He came to my sister's house the day after our day of horror. Because he wanted the decision to be my little brother and I. How could I face the fact of having a father and his body would be alive, but he wouldn't have been the father that you remember. Constantly taking care of him and bathing him as needed. Would have been too much for my 14-year-old mind to handle. I didn't want to him to suffer any longer so I had to make the decision no 14-year-old boy should make. The decision to take my father off life support. My Uncle Mike went there for my answered request. He stood and watched the nurses unplug the machine and saw him take his last deep breath as his chest expanded and his body rose up in to almost a sitting position. Slamming back down to the bed as his soul left his body.

This hurts a whole family and tore apart a community. By father was well known throughout Wilmington. He was like a second father too many children in the community take them around the city his blue station wagon. Taking them to church every Sunday and putting up with the congregation that didn't even want him to be there so they would put us all in the balcony. Segregated from the rest like how they did Black people back in the day. Funny how some of the people back than didn't like him bringing in all the loud trouble youth of Wilmington and complaining even Sunday. Because they were intruding upon the Holy vessel. They act completely different after they heard what happened to my father. Two faced people all around you and I just look upon their faces thinking that I forgot how they acted towards us. But, it wasn't all some people from the Cornerstone Church was on our side and supported to cause he was trying to do for the City of Wilmington. Those are the ones that helped me at the time I needed them. Including Pastor Dunnigan; he stopped by my home and prayed for my family, my brother and I. Years later, Cornerstone welcomed me with open arms. They supplied me with clothes so I can go to work and money for me to catch the DART buses when I had no car. A community should work together and support one another like Cornerstone did for me. But, I guess Donald Cole and Larry Johnson didn't know who they murdered, and as far as they know it was just some guy that was in the way of the goal. They wanted the money my brother Shaheed had and they didn't find it. So we all know what the *street code* is "everybody must go and no witnesses" can be alive to testify. But, I wouldn't allow that to happen, I was going to make it to see the next day. I was alive, but not living. I was walking the earth every day in a zombie like state of mind. They murdered the very person that they named the Benjamin Jones Basketball Tournament after. Children in the city plays in this tournament year after year and fail to realize if it wasn't for him there wouldn't have been a tournament to play in. Nobody ever told them the story because silence in the ghetto is always present. People too afraid to speak up for anything. Silence is a virus in the city that needs to go away. Let's not forget my mother was just as important and they took her off this earth. My mother's brother name was Uncle Butch and he loved his little sister. The pain he felt cracked his heart that was hurting inside like an open wound with salt poured on it. He died 2 months after my mother was murdered. I remember walking down the aisle at the Congo Funeral Home at a slow pace with my head down in my black dress shoes. The red carpet showed my soft footprints behind me with tunnel vision on the sight of the two caskets. My heart beats faster and faster; what scared me the most was watching my cousin in front of me place her hand on my mother's cheek like mother's do to their children as they sleep in their beds at night. Feeling how cold she was, made her explode into tears. Caressing her finger through my mother's hair only to find the bullet hole from when they shot her. Watching my cousin kneels become weak and falling to the ground because reality finally hit her. How could I face to see what she has just seen? I held back my tears, but feeling nothing because this moment is not real this can't be my reality. I see so much death in this life that death no longer scares me. Can you imagine most of your family dying shortly after the murder of your parents? I bet you can't, but if you can imagine. Try to think about what you are doing before you kill a family or a community.

CHAPTER 5

Back to School

My first day back to school was on September 11, 2001. What is the irony in that my first day back to school happened to be on 9-11? The day that was filled with so much tragedy for so many people in the United States. And to be honest, I didn't feel any type of sympathy for the pain everyone was feeling. Until one day a good friend of mines said that even though what happened to me was bad, it's not right to down someone when they're already down. Instead, you should lift people up, stay together and be strong. He was right and for about two weeks the entire country including Wilmington were strong and stuck together. You didn't hear about anybody getting shot, robbed or killed. Everyone had an American Flag hanging in their yards.

So why does something tragic has to happen in order for people to act right? It's because human beings do not respond to nice, but to violence and that's a sad thing to hear. Nevertheless, inside I still didn't care even though my friend had a good point. While everybody around me was soaking in their own tears in my classroom, I was sitting there empty. Everyone was looking at me wondering why I was not upset or crying. Would it have been mean to say that I simply did not care. I probably shouldn't of going back in school so quickly after my parent's death. I clearly needed some mental health and until this day I still haven't received any.

The next few years were one big blur. I can't even remember any of my teacher's names, what classes I was in or even if I did any homework. Looking back, I think I was just going through life floating. Being alive, but not aware of what was going on in my life. During the 9-11 attacks I went to Cab Calloway, which was an art school that my parents got me into two years prior. Not being able to focus became a big problem for me. So my grades dropped drastically and that got me kicked out of school. It was just too much for me to handle with everything going on. And then I had detectives from the police department asking me all these questions, making me relive the night over and over again. For the next few years the police came by less and less, until they didn't come around anymore because they couldn't find any leads on the case. Forcing the Wilmington Police Department to rule it a cold case. It wasn't until my first year in high school that the police came back, I was now 17-years-old. It's a shame for it take Wilmington this long to find anybody. The main problem is because Wilmington didn't have a Homicide Unit back then. They just received a Homicide Unit in 2015. I believe it was not in the budget and the city doesn't want to spend more than it has to protect the people. Everything always boils down to money if you research it long enough. Think about the statement really hard is it cheaper to allow a Black community to kill ourselves than to spend the money preventing us not to? What if an upper middle class community didn't have any police officers around or lack of it; what would happen to their heavenly oasis? I bet their Neighborhoods have Homicide Divisions. Well, it had turned out that the detectives were here because something new came up in the investigation. They found out that it was 3 men involved in the murder of my parents.

    Now at the time of the incident I only saw one person, so this was a total shocker for me. These men were not just involved in what happen on August 31, 2001, but they were also involved in an incident that first occurred on August 22, 2001 on Lancaster Avenue in Wilmington. These men had to be monsters. How could they go around robbing and killing people? The two men entered that house just like they did my house with handguns, intending to steal money and drugs. Again, this happened only 9-days before the murder of my parents. So how could they be so thirsty for blood like sharks? Fear of meeting the men that killed my parents in court filled body. I didn't want any of their family members to come and kill me if they knew that I had something to do with putting them away. I could have felt anger and said fuck them, I'm going make sure these motherfuckers get the death penalty. But, then how could they have realized what they did. Maybe they are just as numb as I am. When it comes to children growing up in the murder capital also known as Wilmington, Delaware who knows how they grew up, who they had to look up to or if they had children? Therefore, the only way they knew how to survive was to rob people in order to get what they want or needed. When you are in that lifestyle you don't realize what your doing is wrong and that you are affecting people lives. You would say fuck them, it's not my friends or family. And why should I care about them, I don't even know them. But, you should know better and if you are a really from Delaware because you know that everybody knows everybody. And if you don't, then there's somebody you know that knows them. So at the time even though I was afraid of what may happen to me, I knew I had to because of loved my parents and justice had to be served. They had to have a punishment so that they would realize what they had done.

During the trial I came face to face with my living nightmares. Their covered faces flickered in my mind every time I closed my eyes. And as I walked up to the witness stand my heart was beating so fast and I was so nervous. Keep in mind, I just came out the bathroom and my nervousness caused me to miss a belt loop on my pants. I looked at the men to my right and I couldn't look them directly in the eye. Even when I tried to see if I recognized them from maybe on the streets of Wilmington. But, I had no idea who they were. All the times when my eyes drifted towards them as they sat behind their desk. All I can see is them laughing at me. I couldn't believe that they thought it was a game. You just murder my parents two years prior and you're laughing. Obviously they either lost their minds or they think this is a game. Maybe they didn't realize the wrong that they have done in their lives at that moment. It's no way that somebody would be willing to face the death penalty knowing that the jury is right there watching them light a hawk in the night. Why would they be willing to meet the Almighty so soon and rot in the fiery depth of hell? Right there I should have just told the state that they deserve the death penalty. But, there was something inside of me that couldn't do that. And I would rather see them spend the rest of their natural lives in prison. Also, I feared that when I died one day that and I'll stand at the Holy Gates and God would ask me why did I decided to ask for them to die. When clearly in His Word it says only He can judge. So I am choosing life because it is better for them. Think about when they are 40 or 60-years-old and they have been in jail for decades, reality will hit and they will finally realize what they have done is wrong and then the guilt will eat them alive. Having guilt is way worse than death. People ask me how could I have made that choice, even when they were laughing at you. I say to them they don't know the gift I just gave to them, but they will one day and if they came

up to me and ask me to forgive them I would say, "Yes, I forgive you."
Matthew 6:14-15
For if you forgive others their trespasses, you're heavenly Father will also forgive you, but if you do not forgive others their trespasses, neither will your Father forgive your trespasses.

Deep down I'm not a monster even though I have the pain that surrounds me and sometimes I feel nothing. I have to show some type of love and compassion even though they don't deserve it.

After that day, my older brother Shaheed Nuriddin felt guilty because he was the one these men were looking for when they broke into our house. He couldn't sleep at night and he would drink heavily even though he was a diabetic. But, I looked at him with love and I didn't blame him. We all make choices, but we don't see the consequences that come with them. A lot of times we think selfishly and nobody matters, but ourselves. Until your mistakes hurt your family and then that's when reality hits. The crazy part in this whole thing is the two men that murdered my parents was his friends. They weren't close friends, but they did hang out from time to time. Their names were Donald Cole and Larry Johnson. I want you to gain an understanding why my brother lived this lifestyle and how it leads up to August 31st.

Eleven years earlier, Shaheed was 14 and once an honor student decided to change his life. This was the time of his life where chasing a dollar and having that good feeling of buying whatever you want when you want it was more important than anything. Other 14-year-olds might be worried about school, but growing up in Wilmington and you watch the friends around you have on the best clothes and have the best girls, and you want that too. Everybody wants to feel like they belong. It's human nature and nobody wants to feel left out. So that made a good boy one of the biggest drug dealers in Wilmington. He didn't know that this would lead to the death of his mother and father In-law. The ones that he thought was his friends, the ones he would have given the clothes off his back for would decide to break into his house and look for him. But, they didn't know that he had moved out the night before. This hurt him to the core. He felt guilty more than vengeful. He felt that if he hadn't been living the hard street life and slinging heroine then his parents would be here today. It was so bad that he would take sleeping pills so that he could sleep at night. Shaheed became so addicted that he would sleep for two days straight and wake up with urine and crap all over him. Until one day, he went into a coma and never came out. He died the day before Christmas. You might as well say he killed himself. He was loved by many people, including his only son. You only get one life to live, so its best you make the right choices. In the Black community it's as if we glorify the lifestyle. When does it end?

On May 1, 2015, I spoken to a close friend of Shaheed's just to get an insight on how everything began. I wanted to gain an understanding of that lifestyle. How can an honor student become consumed by the streets? His response was it all started in 1992 when the movie "Juice" came out. Juice is a 1992 American crime drama thriller directed by Ernest R. Dickerson, written by Ernest R. Dickerson and Gerard Brown. It stars rapper Tupac Shakur and Omar Epps. Additional cast members include Jermaine "Huggy" Hopkins, Khalil Kain, and Samuel L. Jackson; and the film features cameo appearances by Queen Latifah, EPMD, Special Ed,

Ed Lover, Doctor Dré, Flex Alexander, Fab Five Freddy, Yo-Yo, Donald Faison and Treach. The film was directed by cinematographer Ernest R. Dickerson, who has directed and written other Hollywood films such as Surviving the Game and Bulletproof as well as some television series such as ER and The Wire. The film touches on the lives of four youths growing up in Harlem. It follows the day-to-day activities in the young men's lives, starting out as innocent mischief, but growing more serious as time passes by. It also focuses on the struggles that these young men must go through every day as well, such as police harassment, rival neighborhood gangs and their families. This movie made Shaheed and his small group of friends start this lifestyle. They could actually see the characters in the movies as themselves. Running around the streets and basically getting into mischief. Just like children do every day, which is play and get in trouble. My brother's friend said that my brother saw himself as Raheem, which was the pretty boy in the crew, but was also the leader. At the time the movie came out my brother was only 13-years-old. I was in shock that I had to question him because 13-years-old is so young to start selling drugs. It was more of a way to have fun to them and to do the things they wanted to do like travel and go to the beach. Do all the things that more fortunate families would do, like when they took their kids out on vacation to Six Flags and Disney World. Our parents couldn't even afford to go on trips, it was just too many bills going on. Let alone, I was only 3-years-old at the time and my little sister Gloria was just born. She was born with a disability. When she was born her umbilical cord was wrapped around her neck. This caused a lack of oxygen to her brain. So when your parents have two babies it's no time for fun. It was fun having the newest clothes that came out that nobody had yet. Having the exclusive things to get your attention that made you feel popular or important.

He had one person in the streets that he looked up to that did the same things. So he admired him so much that he mimicked him. The guy's name was Jean, which was his older brother on his dad's side. Jean would have a new shirt on and if he got a stain on it he would take a ride to the mall just to buy the same shirt and go get a new pair of socks to wear every day. Due to this, my brother was super fresh and always had the best and newest clothes. I looked up to him myself as I grew up; I guess to me he was like a superstar. Forget Michael Jordan or LeBron James because I had Shaheed Nuriddin. Even time a new gaming console would come out he would buy one for us and himself. Back then a new system would come out like every year and he had so many cars. I never knew where he got the money for all this stuff. I just knew that if I needed a dollar or to get me something from the store he was the person to ask. I'm not going to lie; I know now how easy it is to be sucked into that lifestyle. You see other people with money and you have nothing so you want to me just like them. But, like we all do we look at the good, but we don't see the bad that's on the other side of the rainbow.

A week before my brother died, I think he realized that beginning was the end. Victims of violent crimes hardly tell their stories. They write stories to help other victims of the same type of crimes. Give them ways to get through the trauma that they went through. For example, I was watching Oprah one day and a woman was on there and she was telling her story of how she found out her father was a psychopath and killed so many women. Now what she does is tell her story to many women to help them heal. I'm a victim and I want to help prevent the source of the problem. This will be a hard task to do. I have to try to convince a culture in order to break the cycle. Hopefully my experience can change people. I found out so many things about myself. I know what depression feels like. Imagine living your entire life in third person. Like you created yourself on some video game and you have the joystick. Each level you get to is an accomplishment in your life. But, it feels like you only made it to level 14, but you're on level 27. You can't even remember what happened from level 14 to 27. The levels represent your age and I'm still that 14-year-old boy in the house on 23rd Street. You are watching yourself, but feeling all the pain, but you can't break out. You are trapped inside of your own mind and it feels like it's nobody that can save you. So you cry out for help, hoping that some will save you from yourself. I feel like this now, but somehow I don't know why it has not consumed me. Being this way gave me the ability to understand how people feel because I feel the same way every day like am in a living dream. When I have a little child and doesn't matter if it is male or female; I will make sure they don't get caught up in the lifestyle that most children in the Black community get sucked into, which is robbing, killing and stealing. Because you are people that are not in that life, just like me. But, they are not going to turn out to be a salesman at Raymour and Flanigan making to $50,000 a year. They might turn out to be a killer and not understand why they took a life because they don't value human life. This is a sad reality and we need to change our thinking pattern. For the hope of so many children that grow up in poverty or even worse Wilmington, Delaware. I had to completely separate myself from the dark cloud that is over Wilmington.

Traumatized

After talking with my Uncle Mike, the younger brother of my father Benjamin H. Jones, he convinced me that Georgetown Delaware was a better place to live than where I was currently living. He was right; Georgetown is a lot quieter. So I decided to move in with my uncle.

CHAPTER 6

New Evidence

Days turned into years and before I knew it, its 2003 and sadly I don't even remember the years in between as if I was sitting in a room on pause. Not realizing the world around me was still going on and not really caring about my day to day life. Just sitting and wishing the pain would go away, but it never had. Nothing was important to me any more in this world. Not school, not homework not even taking a shower. My depression on the inside was eating away at my soul like a cancer. The motorized chainsaw inside of me that I called my turmoil ripped me apart, but nobody even noticed because they were too busy worrying about their own lives. Looking back on my life as I sit on my girlfriend porch smoking a Newport. The nicotine smoke fills my lungs calms my nerves as the sound of birds and cars riding on I-95 are in the background soothing me from my traumatized mind. Closing my eyes praying to God for what to do next on this journey that we call life. Fighting trying to remember myself at 17-years-old sitting at my small desk reading this old new Social Studies textbook that smelled like old newspapers. Not even reading the pages my teacher told us to read because there was more amusing message from the students that written on the book before me. Messages that said things like *"Fuck school, I come from the school of hard knocks and teach me how to survive on these streets from the bullets falling in the air when I walk to the corner store."* I read it until the sound of the intercom calls me to the principal's office, "Devon Jones to the office please." So I make my way through the hallway with students standing by the bathrooms making drug transactions.

I arrived at the office and looked through the glass and saw that the 2 detectives from back in 2001 was standing at the front counter. I opened the office door and they turned around to introduce themselves. "Hello Devon do you remember us? I'm Officer Read and this is my partner Santiago." "Yes, I remember," I replied. "I just wanted to inform you that something new has come in the case involving the death of your parents. It was a cold case, but we found some key evidence that opened the case back up and we need you to testify on what you saw on August 31, 2001," Officer Read stated with a confident tone.

This new found information had brought a relief to my heart because I thought they would never find the killer. I thought that I would be forever walking on eggshells every time I walked outside thinking my nightmare would find me and put a bullet in my head as he watched me marinate in my own pool of blood. Then taking two more shots to my chest just to be sure I was dead. We all know that the street code is everybody must go in a home invasion and there can be no witnesses.

One day I was sure they found me when I was walking to the Seven Eleven right down the street from my sister's house in Edgemoore. It was a nice spring day with birds singing in the trees and I wanted a Slurpee. The all blue kind that makes your lips turn so blue it makes it look like you're suffocating. I just wanted to experience my brain freeze fix for the day because Lord knows I was addicted to those things. I was in a steady day dream about my blue Slurpee when I noticed this all black Buick was creeping into the complex. I looked over my shoulder to see who it might be. The Buick pulled beside me and rolled down the window slowly. Whoever was on the passage side looked at me as my eyes locked in with his. The sinister look on his face pierced my soul causing fear to leak out of my vessel. This mystery man pointed his index finger at me and pretended it was gun and pulled the trigger. All I could remember was the smile on his face as I ran all the way back in to my sister's house as fast as I could. I was out of breath by the time I reached her door steps.

Once I got inside my curiosity peeked out her sliding glass door. Watching my hot breath fog up her sliding door; trying not to make the long pearl white blinds move too much to give away where I was hiding. But, when I looked out I saw no one and I don't know if it was someone that was playing games with me or if it was for real. Feeling the need to take myself down her hallway into the bedroom and lay down. Praying over in over the same message, "Please God protect me against all evil." Living in fear is the worst because you are not able to enjoy life. Fearing everything around me, constantly feeling like the walls are boxing me in tighter and tighter. Knowing I was the only one that could tell my story in such a way that my nightmare stays in jail the rest of his nature born life. It was good news because they found out that it was 3 men involved in the murder of my parents.

So at time. even though I was afraid I what may happen to me. I knew I had to testify because of the loved of my parents and justice had to be served. They have to have a punishment so that they realized what they have done. However, everybody is worthy of forgiveness in this world regardless of the sin because to God all sin is the same. Lying, stealing, or hating your neighbor is the as bad as murder. Don't get it confused for what you are reading between this chapter and the last. I want you to realize that both these things are happening at the same time in my mind.

My times and event are shuffled memories similar to the songs that play on random on your iPods. Witnesses' murder put effect on me in the named Dissociative Disorder, which make me escape reality in ways that are involuntary and unhealthy. A person with a dissociative disorder experiences a disconnection and lack of continuity between thoughts, memories, surroundings, actions and identity. The symptoms of dissociative disorders — ranging from amnesia to alternate identities — depend in part on the type you have. Symptoms usually develop as a reaction to trauma and help keep difficult memories at bay. Times of stress can temporarily worsen symptoms, making them more obvious. Dissociative disorders cause problems with functioning in everyday life. Treatment for dissociative disorders may include talk therapy (psychotherapy) and medication. Although treating dissociative disorders can be difficult, many people learn new ways of coping and lead healthy, productive lives. But, coping the only way to cope is to believe on the father of all living things for he guides me through this maze of life in my mind. Understand being traumatized is serious and even though I am alive, but my old soul is dead and that the reason why people say you killed a part of me. This curled world has tarnished my perfect shine and I want you all the slide in and out and experience my confusion in the words of on these pages.

CHAPTER 7

A Family Ripped Apart

Laying down grooving to the sounds of the television entering my ear lobes as weed smoke cloud my lungs. Thinking my pain was worse and no family member that I know can relate to what I experienced. To be honest, they know the reason why they can't because my family was ripped apart by cold blooded murder. They have a totally different prospective than I do. Their prospective is just as bad as my brothers and sisters have been traumatized by their own nightmares from a relationship between my mother and their very own father. Who use to abuse them every day from a young age of five to seven years old? Can you imagine? Oh I forgot, you can't. So I'm going to let you imagine to the point you can absorb it until it becomes your reality. My mother shouldn't have been the one to die to them because of all the abuse she went through her own married life. Knowing and wishing that it was their father that died and they would only go to his funeral in respect of their brothers and sisters, but for him personally they wouldn't even give a fuck. They would cry as they pushed through a heavy door to get to my mother before she slipped the metallic shape razor blade through on yellow bone complexion wrist. While she tried escape the world of her everyday abuser. Feeling just as trapped as I felt in the room I was in when her murderer killed her. She was trapped mentally on the cold floor of that bathroom. Traumatized to the point you wish you were a bird like Jenny from Forest Gump as she kneels in the wide open cornfield with young Forest. They were abused mentally and physically. Watching our mother go through something and they can't be her Superman and Wonder Woman. My sister Diwanya was abused to the point where her father kicked her in to the fire place corner leave a faded scare on the crown of her head. The air escaping her body from the force. Only to fall on the ground into unconsciousness. Our mother was their only angel in their hell. Now she would have to go watch her savior in a body bag and look at her blue pale body for identification. Having a father that beat my brother tony at five years old for accidentally falling on the white sidewalk scraping his knee and crying from the pain. "Why couldn't it had been their father? Why Lord? Why?!" they screamed to the top of their lungs towards the heavens. My mother knew my father 15 years and never married him because she was afraid my father would turn into her ex-husband. Loving my father so much, but living in fear of the past and still ending up dying with the man in a till death do us part statement together side by side in a dark hall way. At least she escaped this hell with love unknowingly. My half brothers and sisters baring his last name Nuriddin. which he created from his Muslim faith. Where their Muhammad was nowhere to be found, but Jesus, surrounded Isaiah and me in that tiny room. So whose God is more powerful? My brother Tony used to take her out every Mother's Day. Now he can't even look at a picture of happy memories of her, trying to purposely suppress every emotion. Locking in back in the far corners of his mind. Yet to find himself to be the one to write his mother's obituary for the news Journal. This story of this family experience of murder shocked our foundation. This story is so deep it gives deep a whole new definition. So are you sure you want to continue to read the deeper you go in the rabbit hole. Proceed with caution of this yellow light. I know you can relate somewhat. Right? It conjures of so much hurt sitting with your family as the tell you stories of the mother they had and a father that they don't claim as a father. Is it better to grow up with a father that was never there for you or a father that was there, but abused you throughout your entire youth? The house on 23rd Street is a house of horror in so many ways. How many tears are soaked in the floor boards and watering the weeds that rest under the foundation of the house. For many families in Wilmington they all have their own houses on hunted hills. My older brother Shaheed slept in the same your room my mother was in before she was murdered. Drinking and taking sleeping pills to cloud his thoughts. Whiles him laying his head on his dark pillow at night. Feeling guilty because he was the one these men was looking for when they broke into our house. The words of my sister Fatima repeat over and over in his mind. It's all your fault moms' dead rip through the air piercing through his heart. But, I looked at him with love I didn't blame him. We all make choices, but we don't see the consequences that come with them. A lot of time we think selfishly and no body matters, but ourselves. Until you heavy mistake hurts your family and then that's when reality hits like a mentor impacting the earth. The crazy part in this whole things is the two men that murdered my parents was his friends. They were close friends, but they did hang out from time to time. I want you to gain an understanding why my brother lived this lifestyle and how it leads up to August 31St

Eleven years earlier Shaheed was 14 and once an honor student, decided to change his life. This was the time of his life where chasing a dollar and having that good feeling of buying whatever you want when you want it was more important than anything. Other fourteen-year-olds might be worried about school. But, growing up in Wilmington and you watch the friends around you have on the best clothes and have the best girls, you would want that to. Everybody wants to feel like they belong. Its human nature and nobody wants to feel left out. So made a good boy one of the biggest drug dealers in Wilmington. He didn't know that this would lead to the death of his mother and father In-law. The ones that he thought was his friends and he would have given them the clothes off his back. Would decide to break into his house and look for him. But, they didn't know that he had moved out the night before. This hurt him to the core. He felt guilty more than vengeful. If felt that he hadn't sold been living the hard street life and slinging Heroine. Than his parents would be here today. It was so bad the he took sleeping pills so that he could sleep at night. Shaheed became so addicted that he would sleep for two days straight and wake up with urine and crap all over him. Until one day he went in a coma and never came out he died the day before Christmas. You might as well say he killed himself. He was loved by many people, including his only son. You only get one life to leave its best you make the right choices. In the Black community it as is we glorify the lifestyle. When does it end?

CHAPTER 8

Suicidal Beginnings

The Wind blows tickling the tiny hairs on my neck as I sit in the cold with no coat nor hat wishing to die as the Devils hot breath speaks in my ear. He is speaking words of negativity, pursuing my subconscious. *Therefore, I thought to myself, "Why is my life full with open wounds of my heart and I'm feeling as though the Lord can't mend my pain?"* I had these thoughts while trying to fight off the burden that I mentally put on myself. Not even realizing that I could possibly die from being in the cold sitting on this Oakwood fence that the park put up in the trailer park in Georgetown.

Living with my Uncle Michael is harder than I thought because in his voice I hear the tone of my father in every breath. I thought it would be easier not living in Wilmington. But it's not because his voice I have to hear it every day and I can't escape August 31, 2001. And now at 17 my teenage mind can't understand because I'm stuck with a feeling of no belonging. I'm pretending to be happy, but in the inside I'm crying pools of sorrow. How can I escape? There isn't any escape, but to die. But even after death, the pain that you feel is still in your heart. So why play along with the thought? Maybe because at least I'm not on earth anymore dealing with this constant reminder.

Hoping someone reads the words of pain I left back on the green kitchen counter because it would give them a look into the future that I was planning for myself. I watched every vehicle riding by and their reflecting lights hoping someone would take the time out to stop to ask how I was doing today. But then the voice of an angel can from out the shadows of my darkness so I lifted up my head slowly as if it was a heavy weight wrapped around my neck. The voice was a woman that barely knew me and she stopped and asked me what I was doing outside in the blistering cold. "Just thinking," I uttered in a stressful tone. Her name was Geneva Upshur.

Sounds of concern left her lips and connected with my deep emotions that were trying to get out. I'm sick of being trapped inside the four corners of my mind. This cloud that is shadowing my calm relaxed mind is thick and heavy and I didn't know how much longer I could hold on. But, this voice…this voice was my hope even though I didn't know what or where it would lead me. "Ej is in the house, if you want to go in the door is unlocked," she said. I knew her son from around the neighborhood so it didn't seem like a bad idea because I wanted to feel better.

So got off the Oakwood fence and walked through the trailer park as the dew from the grass stained my sneakers. And while leading up to the door steps my feet echoed off the steps in loud thumps as I opened the door and walked in to sit in their living room. It just felt so different here as if it was meant for me to be here and I'm not supposed to ever leave. I stayed the entire day and I didn't care whether or not my uncle was worried about me because this place helped me forget my pain. I even offered to help her son Ej clean the house before his mother got back home. Around five o' clock as we were finishing up the dishes and we heard the sound of car tires rolling over gravel and the squeaky brakes coming from outside the door. It was the angel again and she walked in with a smile on her face and looked at me while the blue Dawn soap suds moisturized my hands as the hot water bounced off each dish in the sink.

"Aww you're like a son I never had," she said. What would make her say such a thing? What did she see in me that she wanted to claim me as her son? My heart melted like candle wax to a flame. The warmth gave me life and helped warm my cold heart as my mouth was open in shock and wonder when I looked into her brown eyes. I quickly dried my hands off because I needed to reflect on the emotions I was feeling. Things were becoming clearer than it had been for 3 years. But now I had to go back home to my uncles because it was getting dark and they probably thought I committed suicide like I was planning to do. I wanted to feel my life slipping away from the vessel that God has blessed me with because I felt the hurt this body was feeling and it was too much for me to bare. Maybe running out in front of a car and feeling my rib cage crack as the hot hood of the car burned my dark chocolate skin. Along with my skull hitting the windshield causing it to shatter, would feel better than remembering what I had seen that allows my nightmares to take control of my mind. But, I had to stay strong and continue on with my life. Who knew what would be next for the life of Devon Diwan Jones and how would I know what would be in store for me if I took my life. The only thing that would have been in store would have been a closed casket funeral with my body lying in plush white interior of a fresh pine box. Actually, my entire life was a pine box. So can you blame me for wanting to make it a reality or was it already? I guess I would have just had to ponder that thought as I worked my way back to 27908. As I were walking back, I looked down and kicked every pebble that rubbed the bottom of my shoes. While taking tiny steps, no bigger than half a foot because I knew I didn't want to go back into this house to hear the voice of a man that sound just like my father. My nightmare of what happened in 2001 never leaves my thoughts and to hear my uncle is a constant reminder. So how could I deal with such a thing?

Once I walked through the door all the lights were on in the house and the television was turned down to the point you can hear all the creaks in the floor. I could hear my aunt and uncle getting off the plush mattress and walking towards their bedroom door getting ready to confront me. My uncle opened the door with a hard swing to the point the mirror that was on the living room wall shook. My uncle came out with the walk of my father and my aunt followed behind him. His light skin turned pale red as I knew that he was upset with me because he knew I had been gone for a while. For I have been told time after time to tell them where I was going so that they would at least know where I was if anything would happen to me. I never felt like I had to because if they ever wanted to reach me it's not like they didn't have my cell phone number and I was 18-years-old. My aunt sat onto the couch that was directly across from where I was standing as my uncle continued to stand. He was preparing to give me one of his famous speeches. They didn't know what I was going through at the time. They didn't know I was planning on killing myself that day. Being traumatized is not an easy thing to overcome and my adolescent mind made it even harder to overcome. He told me that he couldn't handle me anymore and that I should just go back to Wilmington with my sister. Why would I want to go back to the city my parents were gunned down? I couldn't handle that type of thing. I began to cry and all my thoughts overwhelmed me as my heavy tears fell onto my shirt. I pleaded with them, "What about school? Can I at least finish?" "You can finish school in Wilmington," he said. Then I quickly replied in an angry tone, "I would rather live with Geneva Upshur!" Then I stormed down the street and I made her fully aware of what was going on and what my uncle was trying to do as far as sending back to the murder capital. She welcomed me with opened arms and I went back to get all my belongings and that's when my life started for the good. I found myself with a family that barely knew me, but adopted me into their family. It was the best thing that ever happen to me. You know the good thing about God is that you never know what direction He will lead you. But, just believe that if you are going through a tough time in your life you got to thank God because something great is coming your way.

James Chapter 1:2-4

Consider it pure joy, my brothers and sisters, [a] whenever you face trials of many kinds, 3 because you know that the testing of your faith produces perseverance. 4 Let perseverance finish its work so that you may be mature and complete, not lacking anything.

CHAPTER 9
No Escaping

Even though my Heaven has reach my reality. Now that I been embraced by the family of Geneva Upshur. The death of loved ones visits my dreams in the darkness behind my eye lids. Waking up in a drizzling cold sweats and deep breathes with a pounding heart. Envisions of the past, which have always been tragic for me. My little sister was always had a smile on her light skinned face even though she went through so much physical agony. Loving her as if she was a normal little girl because to me I never seen her any different. Wilmington did see her different as we walk in to stores like save a lot and would get constant hard stares from adults to adolescents as we walk her in her red stroller. She never paid any attention to them all she did was play with her toys with a laugh that would make you smile. Her name was Gloria Benjamin Jones and she was two years younger than myself. Gloria was forever in a baby state of mind and myself being so young I didn't know. I just thought she was one big baby. My sister was born with a mental disability based on the facts that air couldn't get to her brain when my mother was pregnant with her. Causing my mother to get an emergency c- section otherwise Gloria would have died. There was so many doctors' appointments throughout her short life because she only lived to see the age of nine years old. The sad part about it only she first person I seen pass away in front of my eyes and at the time I was only eleven years old. One day Gloria lost the urge to eat, which was completely unlike her. She was still on the bottle at the age of nine because that was the only way she would eat. Her bottles would be filled with milk or anything just peach flavored oatmeal. So to find that she would eat her favorite was odd and unusual. That same day driving down in our 1980s Mazda 626 with the red interior that had self-belts that were so hot in the summer time that it felt like touching a pot on the stove. No power windows having to roll the windows down by hand. The warm summer air drift into the car as I look to my left look it to Gloria's face. Her smile was gone and she had a blank look while the wind blew through her dark brown hair with Isaiah to the left of her playing with an Iago (a bird from Aladdin) that he stole for the store when he was 4-years-old. I look to right out sound my car window on deep taught as cars ride beside us in traffic in concord pike going towards A.I. DuPont. Arriving at our destination getting out the car with the summer sun cooking us above. Squinting my eyes to keep the sun out my eyes as my father takes Gloria out the car to put her in her stroller and my mother fixes her bang so that she looks presentable. Walking in to the hospital doors and hot heat turns to cool comfort. We had to see what the problem was with my little sister to figure out why she wouldn't eat. As we walk down the halls filled with smiling children and alphabet letter we make it to the doctor's office and sign in a waited patiently for the doctor. Ten minutes later the nurse called us he with her blue teddy bear coved scrubs calling us from the waiting room into the back area so that they can take Gloria's blood pleasure before the doctor arrived. After doing so see left and the doctor arrived and after checking her over and asking what was the issue. The doctor told us that she perfectly fine and maybe she was just feeling a little under the weather, but that no eating part was an issue. They ending up putting a feeding tube through her nose as it went down her throat. Gloria went through weeks and week of eating from a feeding tube that pumped

Pediasure into stomach. Sometimes she would pull the tube out and we had to struggle with her to put it back in. Until one night, when I was helping my father put the yellow feeding tube back into her nose, but something was off because she didn't fight; I thought I was so odd. It scared me to the point that I asked my father is she was okay. "Its fine Devon, she's just tired." I took my father's word and headed up the stairs as my footsteps caused the stairs to creek. Making my way to the to my bedroom to sit in my chair to popped my legs up on the dress and watch cartoons. Trying to debate if I want to do this homework for school or not. Not even five minute in to my show my father tells up the stairs in panic. "Devon!" I run down the stair as fast as I could and almost fell down the stair because I was moving so fast. He told me to go next store and knock on the door and to call 9-1-1. Who would have known this would be my first encounter with Wilmington Emergency Service? I opened the door rapidly and run next store sounds of cricket buzz in my ears and mosquitoes bite my neck as I knock on the neighbor's door with urgency. They answered the door and I call 9-1-1 give the address at the time we lived on 34 Henderson Drive, which a long time ago they called it the horse shoe because of the shape of the street. The horse shoe was part of old riverside and now it all gated up so the Wilmington Police Department can you use the house for police training. Back then police wouldn't even go down that street because it was so bad. But, this day they came quick and thank God maybe she will be okay. My father let Isaiah and I go back into the house as he tried with all his might to resuscitate her on the couch because she stopped breathing. Crackled screams escape his mouth. "Come on baby you can make please!" I watched and I saw her light complexion face beginning to fade. By the time the ambulance came it was too late, she was gone and her arm hanged off the edge of the sofa. The EMTS grabbed her risk, lifted my baby sister up and rolled her away into the ambulance. By the time my mother got home from work she was so heartbroken that she couldn't stop shaking. She had just lost a child and no parent should ever have to see their children die before them. The sounds of crickets gave me flash backs to this night and I can't stand to hear them. So much pain and death has hurt my mind and body that I don't feel it any more. The nightmare is every week and they don't stop; I always find myself trapped on Henderson Drive or East 23rd and there is no escape. These are the memories that I have to live with the rest of my life and if I didn't tell you, you wouldn't even know that I endured so much in my life. God keeps my mind sane as I'm in the mist of my mental insanity. If I didn't meet the Lord Jesus, I would have no one to talk to. If you are one of those people that believe God is not real, I have one question to ask you. Could you live the life of Devon Jones??? The Lord is real just as the air and the air in your lungs are real.

Psalm 34:18
The Lord is near to the brokenhearted and saves the crushed in spirit.

How that is in my tiny bed room that I was able have a sound mind to keep my nightmare outside that door? Protect that life of Isaiah and my own. Pain burdens my heart filled with pine needles pricking its vessels. We have to remember that in ever storm there is an eye. Surrounded by the eyewall, a ring of towering thunderstorms where the most severe weather occurs. In the Lord is peace and comfort and I found him on the day that my father got saved? Benjamin H. Jones just lost his only daughter on this night of unexpected tragedy. A life changing event forcing him to seek the Almighty for answers. Leading his family alongside of him as he feels a void in his beautiful soul. Standing beside him hold a firm head, looking up at him in inspiration as his curls fall besides his face. Closing my eyes to mimic my superman and find what God presence feels like. Forever besides me and he will never leave me regardless how much hurts tortures my soul. Crying as the words soak in this book soak in to the words.

Deuteronomy 31:6

Be strong and courageous. Do not fear or be in dread of them, for it is the Lord your God who goes with you. He will not leave you or forsake you.

Forgiving my Nightmares so that I can heal and heal the lives of you. Selflessness is not of God. The pain needs to come out not only for me, but for you so that you all know how I made it. So that I could tell the youth of this city that the choices you make just don't affect you, but a whole community. If you ever had a nightmare that seemed way too real? A nightmare that feels as if it is happening right then and there! There are only two explanations for this particular dream. One being that it could just a figment of your imagination, and the other being that it is absolutely not a dream, but in fact a tragic reality! I had to come to realization that I was not dreaming on one specific night.

CHAPTER 10

Mental Slavery

Crime in murder town is a big issue based off all constant murders you see from Delaware Online that scrolls on your timeline on social media. I think the main reason of why Black on Black crime is such a big topic is mental slavery. You're probably saying in your mind what the hell is this guy talking about. I personally believe if the Black community would come together as one, we would be the most powerful race on this planet. The reason why we can't proceed to our highest potential is that our mindset is totally off track. By all means, it is not our fault that we don't realize that we are all still slaves. But, it's your fault that you choose not to enlighten your mind on the bigger picture that is happening to us all.

On January 1, 1863, all slaves were set free by an American President; our great grandparents were more than likely born slaves. The way they controlled our bodies was from a mental standpoint. If a slave cannot read or write than that would make it nearly impossible to gain the mindset to know how to outsmart our slave masters.

On December 25, 1712, a man named Willie Lynch delivered a speech along the James River in the colony of Virginia. He was a British slave owner in the West Indies. Below is the speech Willie Lynch Delivered.

(Section 1 Willie Lynch)

"Gentlemen. I greet you here on the bank of the James River in the year of our Lord one thousand seven hundred and twelve. First, I shall thank you, the gentlemen of the Colony of Virginia, for bringing me here. I am here to help you solve some of your problems with slaves. Your invitation reached me on my modest plantation in the West Indies, where

Traumatized

I have experimented with some of the newest and still the oldest methods for control of slaves. Ancient Rome's would envy us if my program is implemented. As our boat sailed South on the James River, named for our illustrious king, whose version of the Bible we cherish, I saw enough to know that your problem is not unique. While Rome used cords of wood as crosses for standing human bodies along its highways in great numbers, you are here using the tree and the rope on occasions. I caught the whiff of a dead slave hanging from a tree, a couple miles back. You are not only losing valuable stock by hangings, you are having uprisings, and slaves are running away, your crops are sometimes left in the fields too long for maximum profit, you suffer occasional fires, and your animals are killed. Gentlemen, you know what your problems are; I do not need to elaborate. I am not here to enumerate your problems; I am here to introduce you to a method of solving them. In my bag here, I have a full proof method for controlling your Black slaves. I guarantee every one of you that if installed correctly it will control the slaves for at least 300 hundreds years. My method is simple. Any member of your family or your overseer can use it. I have outlined a number of differences among the slaves; and I take these differences and make them bigger. I use fear, distrust and envy for control purposes. These methods have worked on my modest plantation in the West Indies and it will work throughout the south. Take this simple little list of differences and think about them. on top of my list is "age" but it's there only because it starts with an "a." the second is "color" or shade, there is intelligence, size, sex, sizes of plantations, status on plantations, attitude of owners, whether the slaves live in the valley, on a hill, east, west, north, south, have fine hair, course hair, or is tall or short. Now that you have a list of differences, I shall give you an outline of action, but before that, I shall assure you that distrust is stronger than trust and envy stronger than adulation, respect or admiration. The Black slaves after receiving this indoctrination shall carry on and will become self-refueling and self-generating for hundreds of years, maybe thousands. Don't forget you must pitch the old Black male vs. the young Black male, and the young Black male against the old Black male. You must use the dark skin slaves vs. the light skin slaves, and the light skin slaves vs. the dark skin slaves. You must use the female vs. the male and the male vs. the female. You must also have you white servants and over- seers distrust all Blacks. But, it is necessary that your slaves trust and depend on us. They must love, respect and trust only us."

Everything that Willie said still holds true till this very day. The Black community has not gotten out of the slave mentality. I will break it down on how you are still a slave and how this makes the Black community has self-destructed itself. We have lost our sense of unity and we need to get it back.

The first thing Lynch spoke about is distrust. Making us hate ourselves based on certain characteristics. Age and color were the first two ways he promoted distrust between ourselves along with fine hair, coarse hair, tall or short. Let's think how distrust still runs in today's world. How many times where you were in school and you see other Black people make fun of someone that is too dark or too light. Sometimes I have personally seen females in school being hated by other females because their hair was longer and theirs was shorter and they had to go around where different weaves and styles. Mostly because there are some females think they are better than the rest because one sees them as prettier than the other. Their many passages from Chicago now that many Black women talk about how they hate being Black. One stated... *I hate being Black because every time I like a man, he tells me he doesn't date dark skin women, but he is willing to have sex with me...*

The funny about that her passage is that my fiancée and I prefer light skinned people, but we are both dark skinned. This is probably because of the way we have been programed for generations. Just think about most of the Black celebrities you see on your HD digital boxes has a light complexion. It's like we were taught that being light is beautiful and dark is not. I always loved the beauty of light only because my mother was light-skinned. But, I was always too afraid to approach any of them because I believed most of them were stuck up and that they were the best thing God created. Just to think that I have influenced by a principal Willie Lynch set so long ago. When the lighter colored slaves were allowed to be on the porch or in the homes of their slave masters, causing a divide of hate between two different colors of people. There is power in unity and without it you are weak.

Psalms 133:1
Behold, how good and pleasant it is when brothers dwell in unity.

One example on how hate is a cancer in Wilmington that eats away at us like a parasite. Making it the exact opposite substance of unity. If some was being made fun for being too Black and that person felt like they were being disrespected. So they decide to fight this bully, but the bully doesn't fight back, but decides to shoot instead because he would rather pull out his gun than let somebody beat him up and being labeled a punk. This kind of scenario happens every day and you no longer look at your fellow Black brother or sister as a person, but as some that can ruin your reputation. Before you know it another life is lost to the hard knock streets of Wilmington Delaware. This is the trick that Willie placed on the Black community and we have to find a way to reverse it. The fact of that matter is, I don't think we ever will because it will only get worse because the Bible tells us so.

(Section 2 Willie Lynch)

"Therefore, if you break the female mother, she will break the offspring in its early years of development and when the offspring is old enough to work, she will deliver it up to you, for her normal female protective tendencies will have been lost in the original breaking process. For example, take the case of the wild stud horse, a female horse and an already infant horse and compare the breaking process with two captured nigger males in their natural state, a pregnant nigger woman with her infant offspring. Take the stud horse, break him for limited containment. Completely break the female horse until she becomes very gentle, whereas you or anybody can ride her in her comfort. Breed the mare and the stud until you have the desired offspring. Then you can turn the stud to freedom until you need him again. Train the female horse whereby she will eat out of your hand, and she will in turn train the infant horse to eat out of your hand also. When it comes to breaking the uncivilized nigger, use the same process, but vary the degree and step up the pressure, so as to do a

complete reversal of the mind. Take the meanest and most restless nigger, strip him of his clothes in front of the remaining male niggers, the female, and the nigger infant, tar and feather him, tie each leg to a different horse faced in opposite directions, set him afire and beat both horses to pull him apart in front of the remaining nigger. The next step is to take a bull whip and beat the remaining nigger male to the point of death, in front of the female and the infant. Don't kill him, but put the fear of God in him, for he can be useful for future breeding."

<u>The Breaking Process of the African Woman</u>

Take the female and run a series of tests on her to see if she will submit to your desires willingly. Test her in every way, because she is the most important factor for good economics. If she shows any sign of resistance in submitting completely to your will, do not hesitate to use the bull whip on her to extract that last bit of resistance out of her. Take care not to kill her, for in doing so, you spoil good economic. When in complete submission, she will train her off springs in the early years to submit to labor when they become of age. Understanding is the best thing. Therefore, we shall go deeper into this area of the subject matter concerning what we have produced here in this breaking process of the female nigger. We have reversed the relationship in her natural uncivilized state she would have a strong dependency on the uncivilized nigger male, and she would have a limited protective tendency toward her independent male offspring and would raise male off springs to be dependent like her. Nature had provided for this type of balance. We reversed nature by burning and pulling a civilized nigger apart and bull whipping the other to the point of death, all in her presence. By her being left alone, unprotected, with the male image destroyed, the ordeal caused her to move from her psychological dependent state to a frozen independent state. In this frozen psychological state of independence, she will raise her male and female offspring in reversed roles.

For fear of the young males' life she will psychologically train him to be mentally weak and dependent, but physically strong. Because she has become psychologically independent, she will train her female off springs to be psychological independent. What have you got? You've got the nigger women out front and the nigger man behind and scared. This is a perfect situation of sound sleep and economic. Before the breaking process, we had to be alertly on guard at all times."

Willie believed that if they kept an eye on the thoughts of the Black woman. Then she will teach her offspring in such a way that she would mold the Black male to grow up in a way they wanted us to be, which is obedient. The Black woman will shift her dependency from her Black male companion and toward her offspring so that they will only obey their slave master. Just think about how a child would be born without a male image to look up to, forcing the child to only look up to their mother. Doesn't this sound familiar to what's going on in our community? We see it every day in the ghetto, the streets, the projects or what every slang you want to put on it. It's sad that most Black men and women's lives are some "Dear Momma" song that Tupac song that came out in 1995. Then we have the independent woman, which is the title that most of love the most. But, how are you independent when some of you are so dependent on government assistance like EBT, or WIC that you no longer need a male figure in your life. So you have children was no male figure and the cycle continues over and over. Taking the Black male out of the equation by sending him to jail for not paying child support. This is all just a modernized version of what Lynch talked about. We all slaves and we were never set free. We have been tricked by of government to believe that we are, but by definition "Free" means not under the control or in the power of another. So based on that how are you free? Once we come together and gain some type of unity than the murder rate in the Black community will go down in Wilmington. We put the blame on our mayor and the police, but the problem is ourselves. We have a slave state of mind. So ask yourself how we can fix something that has been messed up for generations. Otherwise there are going to be more murders and more traumatized children who will witness murder just like we did.

CHAPTER 11

Recognize

Due to the fact that we are still in our slave state, trapped inside the roadblock in our minds to only see things one way instead of the bigger picture. We fail to recognize who our real slave master, which is our government. So many things have been set in place to control and to suck money out of our community. Making our community a gateway for drugs and violence. All these factors play a role into why my parents had to be murdered and why so many children are traumatized. My outcome came from my older brother being in a lifestyle that he was lured into based on the environment that he was born is causing him to befriend people of that life of crime and drugs. How did these influences get into Wilmington in the first place? I found out in my journey of enlightenment that it all started with the relationship between the United States and Cuba. The truth was brought to light by one journalist and his name was Gary Webb. After Gary found out what our government was doing to the Black community he was found dead with two gun shots in his head, but they ruled it a suicide because he knew too much. Every person in American history that helped Blacks in some type of way has been murdered. If the truth comes to light than they discredit you in every type of way and then they kill you. They made a movie out Gary Web called Kill the Messenger and after the movie came out they are trying to discredit the movie too. Just look at the article The Washington sent about him:

GARY WEBB WAS NO JOURNALISM HERO, DESPITE WHAT 'KILL THE MESSENGER' SAYS:

By Jeff Leen October 17, 2014

Jeff Leen is The Washington Post's Assistant Managing Editor for Investigations.

An extraordinary claim requires extraordinary proof. That old dictum ought to hang on the walls of every journalism school in America. It is the salient lesson of the Gary Webb affair. It might have saved his journalism career, though it would have precluded his canonization in the new film "Kill the Messenger."

The Hollywood version of his story — a truth-teller persecuted by the cowardly and craven mainstream media — is pure fiction. But, Webb was a real person who wrote a real story, a three-part series called "Dark Alliance," in August 1996 for the San Jose Mercury News, one of the flagship newspapers of the then-mighty Knight Ridder chain. Webb's story made the extraordinary claim that the Central Intelligence Agency was responsible for the crack cocaine epidemic in America. What he lacked was the extraordinary proof. But at first, the claim was enough. Webb's story became notable as the first major journalism cause célèbre on the newly emerging Internet. The Black community roiled in anger at the supposed CIA perfidy.

Then it all began to come apart. The New York Times, The Washington Post and the Los Angeles Times, in a rare show of unanimity, all wrote major pieces knocking the story down for its overblown claims and undernourished reporting.

Gradually, the Mercury News backed away from Webb's scoop. The paper transferred him to its Cupertino bureau and did an internal review of his facts and his methods. Jerry Ceppos, the Mercury News's executive editor, wrote a piece concluding that the story did not meet the *newspaper's standards — a courageous stance, I thought. "We oversimplified the complex issue of how the crack epidemic in America grew," Ceppos wrote. "Through imprecise language and graphics, we created impressions that were open to misinterpretation."*

Jeremy Renner plays Gary Webb in "Kill the Messenger." (Chuck Zlotnick/Focus Features)

Webb resigned and wrote a book defending his reporting. The mainstream press, now known as the legacy media, which had vilified him and which he had vilified in turn, never employed him again. He worked as an investigator for a legislative committee in California and finally for an alternative weekly in Sacramento. He had money troubles and other problems, and ended up taking his own life at 49 in December 2004.

I had a ringside seat to the Webb saga. As an investigative reporter covering the drug trade for the Miami Herald, also a Knight Ridder newspaper, I wrote about the explosion of cocaine in America in the 1980s and 1990s, and the role of Colombia's Medellin Cartel in fueling it.

Beginning in 1985, journalists started pursuing tips about the CIA's role in the drug trade. Was the agency allowing cocaine to flow into the United States as a means to fund its secret war supporting the contra rebels in Nicaragua? Many journalists, including me, chased that story from different angles, but the extraordinary proof was always lacking.

Finally, in April 1989, the U.S. Senate subcommittee on terrorism, narcotics and international operations, chaired by Sen. John Kerry (D-Mass.), weighed in. After an exhaustive three-year investigation, the committee's report concluded that CIA officials were aware of the smuggling activities of some of their charges who supported the contras,

Traumatized

but it stopped short of implicating the agency directly in drug dealing.

That seemed to be the final word on the matter. And then Gary Webb came along.

I was in the Miami Herald's newsroom when the rumble came across that the Mercury News had finally nailed the CIA-cocaine story, proving that the CIA was involved in the cocaine trade and, more significantly, that the agency was responsible for the U.S. crack epidemic. I was astonished — and envious. Until I read Webb's story.

The first thing I looked for was the amount of cocaine that the story said "the CIA's army" had brought into the country and funneled into the crack trade. It turned out to be relatively small: a ton in 1981, 100 kilos a week by the mid-1980s, nowhere near enough to flood the country with crack.

I was also eager to see exactly how he linked the CIA to the cocaine trafficking. (The online presentation of the articles memorably showed a crack pipe superimposed on the agency's seal.) Was he talking about CIA officers, who are employees of the agency, or CIA agents, who are hired foreign contractors? Or subcontractors? Did he name or quote any of them? Did he have any documents?

What he had was this: the testimony of Oscar Danilo Blandon Reyes, described as a former contra leader and drug dealer. Blandon claimed that the leader of his contra group, who was on the CIA payroll, had said, "The ends justify the means." In Blandon's words, "So we started raising money for the contra revolution." Blandon's lawyer told Webb: "Was he involved with the CIA? Probably." Webb also wrote that Blandon's boss had been accused by a witness at his Nicaragua drug trial of participating *in a drug ring that flew cocaine into a U.S. Air Force base in Texas, though the base was not named.*

There was no response from the CIA in the story. But the claims Gary made, man, were they extraordinary:

"For the better part of a decade, a San Francisco Bay Area drug ring sold tons of cocaine to the Crips and Bloods street gangs of Los Angeles and funneled millions in drug profits to a Latin American guerrilla army run by the U.S. Central Intelligence Agency, a Mercury News investigation has found.

"This drug network opened the first pipeline between Colombia's cocaine cartels and the Black neighborhoods of Los Angeles, a city now known as the 'crack' capital of the world. The cocaine that flooded in helped spark a crack explosion in urban America and provided the cash and connections needed for L.A.'s gangs to buy automatic weapons."

And this: *"Thousands of young Black men are serving long prison sentences for selling cocaine — a drug that was virtually unobtainable in Black neighborhoods before members of the CIA's army started bringing it into South-Central in the 1980s at bargain-basement prices."*

In the business, these are called nut graphs, and they are the hardest things for an investigative reporter to write. You must summarize the sometimes bewildering facts you have uncovered, however incomplete or contradictory, and synthesize them into a picture that makes sense. That is what Webb did. And he went too far.

As the Mercury News was first coming under criticism for his reporting, and while the story was the hottest one in the country, an appeal went out to other Knight Ridder newspapers to pick up his *journalism. I was asked to evaluate his reporting for my bosses at the Herald. The Herald did not publish Webb's work.*

After Webb was transferred to Cupertino, I debated him at a conference of the Investigative Reporters and Editors organization in Phoenix in June 1997. He was preternaturally calm. While investigative journalists are usually bundles of insecurities and questions and skepticism, he brushed off any criticism and admitted no error. When asked how I felt about it all, I said I felt sorry for him. I still feel that way.

Webb's supporters point to a 1998 report by CIA Inspector General Frederick Hitz as vindication, because it uncovered an agency mind-set of indifference to drug-smuggling allegations. Actually, it is more like the Kerry committee's report on steroids: "We have found no evidence in the course of this lengthy investigation of any conspiracy by CIA or its employees to bring drugs into the United States," Hitz said. "...There are instances where CIA did not, in an expeditious or consistent fashion, cut off relationships with individuals supporting the Contra program who were alleged to have engaged in drug trafficking activity or take action to resolve the allegations."

Significantly, the report found no CIA relationship with the drug ring Webb had written about.

Webb could draw a Pyrrhic victory from Hitz's report. His work and the controversy it engendered forced the CIA to undertake one of the most extensive internal investigations in its history. Jack Blum, the special counsel who led the investigation for the Kerry committee, said after Webb's death that even though Webb got many of the details "completely wrong," he had at least succeeded in focusing attention on the issue.

But, investigative reporting is unforgiving to those who get it only partially right, especially on their core claims. When a story gets that big, it invites scrutiny and criticism. And criticism of the criticism. Where does it all land in the end? The criticism of the criticism usually fails to come to grips with the salient point: No matter what you think of the CIA, there's no putting the crack-epidemic genie back in the bottle.

You don't have to believe me or Ceppos, or anybody else from the mainstream media on this one. These are the words of Nick Schou, the OC Weekly editor who wrote the book that serves as the basis, with Webb's book, for the movie: "'Dark Alliance' contained major flaws of hyperbole that were both encouraged and ignored by his editors, who saw the story as a chance to win a Pulitzer Prize," Schou wrote in the Los Angeles Times in 2006. On the crack explosion claim: "The story offered no evidence to support such sweeping conclusions, a fatal error that would ultimately destroy Webb, if not his editors."

Despite his facade of certainty, Webb must have known this better than anyone. In his book he took pains to distance himself from the crack claim. "I never believed, and never wrote, that there was a grand CIA conspiracy behind the crack plague," he wrote. "... The CIA couldn't even mine a harbor without getting its trench coat stuck in its fly."

Webb also admitted to mistakes in the execution of the story — though he put the blame on his editors, who he said requested "an increased emphasis on CIA involvement." He said he rewrote those nut graphs at their insistence.

As for "Kill the Messenger," the best that can be said for the movie is that Jeremy Renner gives a spirited performance in a fantasy version of the story in which everyone is wrong, but Gary Webb. It would take an article longer than this one to point out the many departures from what really happened.

Webb will be lionized by some, and the simple story will get told and retold that the mainstream press and his management betrayed him, threw him under the bus. Many people will believe it. Hollywood was making movies about U.S. government cocaine trafficking as early as 1988. Go ahead and rent "The Last of the Finest" or "Above the Law," if you can find them on Netflix. In the age of waterboarding and Edward Snowden, widespread CIA cocaine trafficking seems not only plausible, but downright antiquated.

Before seeing the movie this past week, I hadn't thought much about Webb in a long time. Mostly, he stands out in my mind as a cautionary tale, a warning, especially for the younger reporters on my staff, to keep the hype out of their nut graphs.

The Washington Post wrote this because that this movie might bring up more questions that they didn't want to answer. They our government put these drugs in our community and Wilmington is just one of those cities. Just so they can use us to make money to support their wars. Billions and billions of dollars get made off drugs. I hope you don't this off that money the police get from drug bust gets burned. First, they make from when we sale the drug and then they make money off all the Black people in jail. All evil that is done in this world is because of the money. The Black race has been the driving force of the United States. Showing that me and you are still slaves. Why kill your fellow man for money that you know you not going to able to keep is my point. Get it together Wilmington because there is no reason we can't even walk down our own street without getting shot or stabbed. I just want Wilmington to think about this book long and hard and hope it haunts your dreams at night. Your simple minded thinking will not get you out of this reality you are forced to live in because of drugs or the bad choices your parents decided to make. Dice games on the block for hard gambles and extra cash flow. But you're taking a gamble on your life because you are playing a game with the Devil on his black top filled with trash and old Arizona cans. Every dollar hitting the ground next the Timberland boot of the one sizing you up and trying to see just how much money you have in your pockets. His mind not on this dice game, but on you because I don't think you are making it home to your queen size. You could have been planning on hitting off that side chick that was blowing you iPhone up all day. Thinking about that hard blow from her supple lips. Too bad the only blow coming to you is the sound of the canon once you turn down 30th and Washington. Pay attention Wilmington because you are paying attention to the wrong things. Pay attention to the more important things in life like love for your fellow man. Get off the streets young boy this is your warning book. Your father was supposed to be your role model. Showing you how a man is supposed to conduct himself and leads his family in safety. The word father might not have been in your vocabulary, but it's definitely on the tongues of the children you might have brought into this cruel world. How are you leading them in safety if it's not safe out here for you? There are wolves out here. If they can't get to you because you're lurking in the shadows like Batman. Then they can get to your heart, which is your family. Go to the cemetery and ask my parents because they were a part of the deadly equation of the street life. Your mom is not safe when she walks out her door on her way to her car. She could turn out a result of your wrongdoings. In murder town these streets are shooting everything moving. Women, children and men to the point where it might not even be a gunshot be a car hitting you on a hit and run. There's no light in your darkness. They told Caroline not to walk towards the light on poltergeist. But, I suggest you walk towards the light. All light is good and in the light is happiness and joy. The only light that isn't it the kind that comes off the barrel on the semi-automatic that you might meet right after reading this chapter. For in board day light the darkness of your eyes lids you will see causing the tears run down from all that know of you. Don't you think that it's enough tears that water the weed growing in between the crack of all Wilmington or any other Black community you go to? Don't be the next one of a R.I.P shirt and celebrated by teddy bears and candle light once the Sun goes down. If your mission is to be a hot celebrity and remembered only on anniversaries of your death, then keep on the same path and one day that day shall come. No amount of alcohol poured on the spot where you were gunned down can bring you back to give your family a hug that one last time. And giving your mother, her last kiss on the cheek because to me it seems like your mind has been made up Wilmington and you will forever be traumatized.

PHOTOS

ADD YOUR OWN SELFIE

Dear Reader,

Please take your own "Selfie" and place it in the picture frame above holding your copy of "Traumatized" then place it on Facebook and or Instagram

Thanks,

    Devon

www.ingramcontent.com/pod-product-compliance
Lightning Source LLC
Chambersburg PA
CBHW070549300426
44113CB00011B/1832